The Grounds ot
MANCHESTER CITY

Clowes Street 1880 to the City of Manchester Stadium

By David Burton

Published 2005 by arima publishing

www.arimapublishing.com

ISBN 1-84549-046-0

Printed and bound in the United Kingdom

Typeset in Garamond 12/14

arima publishing
ASK House, Northgate Avenue
Bury St Edmunds, Suffolk IP32 6BB
t: (+44) 01284 700321

www.arimapublishing.com

To

Daniel and Megan

Ride the rollercoaster & wear the badge with pride, love Dad xxx

The Grounds of
MANCHESTER CITY

1:   CLOWES STREET 1880-1881

The history of Manchester City Football Club can be traced back to 1880 and the church of St Marks, West Gorton. The Reverend Arthur Connells daughter- Miss G Connell, had an idea to initially form a 'workingmens club' with a cricket team, then a football team to benefit the men folk of the congregation, and hopefully lead them away from a life of disrepute.

Two church wardens- Messrs Beastow and Goodyeare were set the task to establish the football team. They soon got together enough players to entertain other local teams of the day in friendly matches during the 1880-81 season, despite the fact that football was not the most popular sport in Manchester at that time but rugby. In other lancashire towns however, football was proving to be the sport that caught the imagination of men folk- both young and old.

St Marks Church was situated on Clowes Street between William Street and Robert Street, with a parish school built at the rear. The area was typically Victorian, with rows of 'Coronation Street' style terraced houses on muddy roads. Almost all the people living there would have worked and socialised locally, certainly the 'Brooks and Doxeys Union Iron Works' situated just a stones throw away employed Messrs Beastow and Goodyeare as executives, and it seems many of the players were employees as well as congregation members. In fact two of Beastows sons played in the first match.

Also important was that the Iron Works Company owned spare land just off Clowes Street, which was unused and sufficient for a football pitch, even though it was probably no more than a plot of rough ground. It seems probable that the land was already being used by the cricket team set up as part of the workingmen's club.

St Marks Church, Clowes Street, West Gorton

However, it was enough to get started and is almost certainly the venue for St Marks first match which took place on Saturday 13th November 1880 against the Baptist Church (Macclesfield). Twelve players played for each side- not unusual in 1880, and the players who featured for St Marks (West Gorton), as they were known were:

Charles Beastow, John Beastow, W Chew, J Collinge, W Downing, H Heggs, Frederick Hopkinson, Richard Hopkinson, E Kitchen, A McDonald,

J Pilkington and W Sumner (Team Captain).

The game ended 1-2 for Baptist Church (Macclesfield).

Just two weeks later another game took place at Clowes Street with St Marks drawing 0-0 with Harpurhey team 'Arcadians'. At least five other games took place during that first season, culminating in March 1881 with victory away against Stalybridge Clarence.

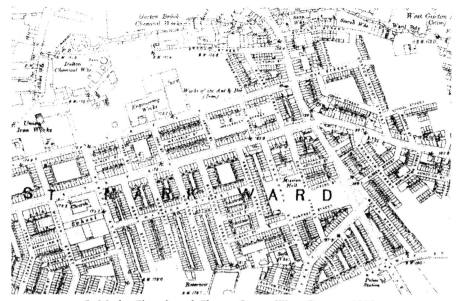

St Marks Church and Clowes Street, West Gorton, 1893.
The site of the pitch was adjacent to the Union Iron Works.

St Marks (West Gorton) played for only one season at this venue, indicating its poor state and the ambitions of the club to progress to better things. Obviously basic and rough ground, certainly not enclosed, it did however sow the seeds for the club we know and love today. St Marks church was sadly demolished in the mid 1970s some years after the terraced houses around it had already gone during the slum clearances of the late sixties and early seventies.

Clowes Street still proudly bears its name today, however it has been re-routed from its original straight path from Hyde Road to Gorton Lane, and it is now in two parts, separated by the A6010 dual carriageway (Pottery Lane), which continues via Alan Turing Way.

Clowes Street is less than a mile from the City of Manchester Stadium, the club certainly 'came home' when moving from Maine Road in 2003.

9

After the first season at Clowes Street, St Marks (West Gorton) opted for a move to nearby Kirkmanshulme Cricket Club on Redgate Lane. Approximately 5 acres in size and adjacent to Belle Vue Zoological Gardens, the venue offered a much improved playing surface and a pavilion for spectators. This move reflected the ambitious nature of the club and would have been instrumental in attracting new players.

As new players arrived from outside the parish, the church decided in November 1881 to remove its patronage. The consequence of this was an immediate name change to West Gorton (St Marks). Many parishioners did however continue to support and play for the club. Certainly, without their fundraising efforts, organisation and ability to attract opposition, the club would never have survived these early days.

1881-82 proved a successful season at the cricket club, in which twelve friendly matches were played. Most notable was a 2-1 home victory over Newton Heath. The attendance that day was reported as being 'around 5,000', although no evidence exists to confirm that this is correct. It does however show the popularity of the club around the Gorton area.

Kirkmanshulme Cricket Club was bordered to the north by a railway line with Belle Vue Avenue to the south. In the south-eastern corner was the pavilion building, which if typical of victorian cricket pavilions would have housed changing facilities for the players, a bar area, office and a small covered seating and standing area. Behind this pavilion and just outside the ground was the Longsight Hotel and entrance to the zoological gardens.

The game against Newton Heath proved to be the last football match played at the ground. At the end of the season the cricket club asked

West Gorton (St Marks) to leave and find a new home for the following season. Substantial damage had been caused to the playing surface and whether this was caused by players or the spectators who attended the final game nobody knows.

Aerial photograph dated 1937 showing the site of Kirkmanshulme Cricket Club, Queens Road ground, Greenwood House flats on Pink Bank Lane, Belle Vue Speedway stadium and Belle Vue Greyhound stadium.

What is a fact however was that the club was just two years old and required its third home. West Gorton (St Marks) became desperate for a pitch in the area. Gorton was expanding rapidly with new factories, improving transport links and an increasing population. These factors made securing a new ground all the more difficult.

The search for a new home after just one season at Kirkmanshulme Cricket Club ended when West Gorton (St Marks) made the short journey to Queens Road. This move was not a step forward however, but one forced upon the club.

Just half-a-mile from Clowes Street was a patch of land which was reputably being used to graze animals yet was deemed fit to play football on. Known locally as 'Clemington Park' or 'Donkey Common', the club was obviously pleased just to have secured somewhere to play no matter how poor, although this setback after playing to large crowds at the cricket club must have been demoralising.

Gorton Park, formerly Clemington Park or Donkey Common. This was the Queens Road ground.

During 1882-83 season the club played nine matches but only had a full team in three of those games. Possibly the enforced move played a part, the poor state of the ground or maybe the lack of patronage following the church's withdrawal the year before. Whatever it was the club was clearly battling to survive. In truth, the venue at Queens Road was probably no better than what the club had left at Clowes Street, and the pitch would have required work to bring it up to a reasonable standard. The most notable feature of the surroundings would have been the large spice mill adjacent- not to mention the smell!

For the second season at the ground, 1883-84, West Gorton (St Marks) merged with another local side- Gorton Athletic, who were homeless. The club retained the name of West Gorton (St Marks). On the pitch the team faired better winning seven of the eight games played that season. One match, a home victory over Furness Vale attracted a crowd of 1,000. Although impressive for an open ground, it was still someway short of the attendance against Newton Heath some two years earlier.

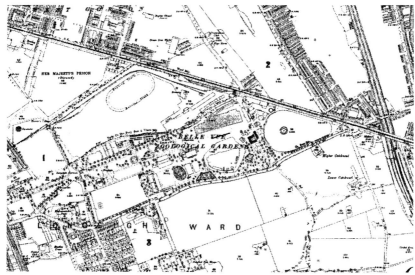

The locations of three grounds are visible on this map of the Belle Vue area of Gorton, 1893. The Kirkmanshulme Cricket Club (1), Queens Road (2) and Pink Bank Lane (3) grounds. Note also the running track, which became the speedway stadium.

Off the pitch however the merger was not working and following constant problems the club decided to go it alone and move ground again, leaving athletic to play under their old name. Mssrs Beastow, Chew and Kitchen decided to rename the club Gorton Association Football Club.

The Queens Road ground is still bordered by Hyde Road to the south. Queens Road led from here along the grounds eastern side and continued to Gorton Lane. This road has mostly been redeveloped although Queensland Road followed its route for a small distance. Manchester Council acquired the ground in 1891 and it has never been built upon. It is now known as Gorton Park.

4:   PINK BANK LANE 1884-1885

The newly named Gorton AFC joined the Manchester & District Football Association during the 1884-85 season. In October agreement was reached to play at Pink Bank Lane- another plot of rough ground, on the corner with Kirkmanshulme Lane.

The vacant plot of land was found by young forward Lawrence Furniss, a man who was to become an important figure in the history of the club over the next fifty years.

Aerial photograph taken in 1926. Pink Bank Lane ground is at the bottom right.

An annual rent of £6 was agreed with the landowners and Gorton AFC began to organise fixtures at their new home, although their season was starting a little late.

This one and only season at Pink Bank Lane proved to be a success. The club, with its new association status, played 16 games winning 7. Finances were stabilised and the club were aware that a good ground was essential for the success of the club, so it seems that Pink Bank Lane was always a stopgap measure until more suitable premises were found.

Pink Bank Lane was essentially no different to Clowes Street or Queens Road. It was an open field which would not of been ideally suited to football and probably required work to make playable. Therefore, after just one season, the club were once again on the move.

Some years later the 'Greenwood House Flats' were built on this site then subsequently demolished. It has since been redeveloped once again.

5: REDDISH LANE 1885-1887

During the close season of 1885 Gorton AFC found new premises at Reddish Lane. This involved a move to the eastern side of Gorton and thus became the closest that the club has ever been to moving outside Manchester, for the ground was situated just inside the city boundary. It is also a ground which is frequently overlooked in the clubs history, for many researchers omit this venue completely, instead giving the club a three year tenure at Pink Bank Lane.

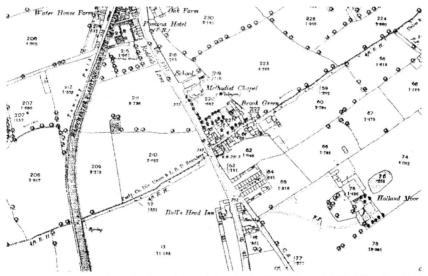

Reddish Lane showing the location of the Bulls Head Inn, 1893. The football ground is believed to have been beside this public house.

However, the Reddish Lane ground did exist and the club played there for two seasons from 1885.

Once again the agreed rental payment was £6 per annum. On this occasion the landowner was also the landlord of the 'Bulls Head Inn'. This payment included use of the public house for players changing facilities.

Although the pitch was once described as being 'in very bad condition', it was still most probably the best venue in the area at that time. Again the pitch would not have been enclosed, although Gorton AFC attracted an attendance of 1,500 to one cup-tie against Gorton Villa during the 1886-87 season.

The club at this time was still in its early days, but the constant upheaval and effort required in finding new premises to play was hampering progress and a new long term home was really required. After two seasons at Reddish Lane the landlord proposed a rental increase, so when club captain K McKenzie took a short cut across some waste ground alongside the railway arches at Bennett Street, near Hyde Road, and realised that the area could be developed into a pitch and fully enclosed football ground, the timing was perfect. It was also a move back towards the clubs traditional base of West Gorton.

The Bulls Head Inn was later demolished and replaced with the Bulls Head Hotel in 1906.

As for the football club, well they would never look back again.

The club had found itself moving again after two years at Reddish Lane and a name change to 'Ardwick Association Football Club' followed. The next step would be professionalism, major changes that would propel the club towards the football league.

City 2 Middlesbrough 1, at Hyde Road, 14th April 1911. Note the multi-spanned roof.

The patch of land discovered by club captain McKenzie was owned by the Manchester, Sheffield & Lincolnshire Railway Company. A meeting between the company and club secretary Walter Chew ended with the clubs agreement to pay £10 rent for seven months tenancy from August 1887. The ground would be enclosed but very cramp. It also required immediate work but this was nothing new to the club. Galloway's works bordered the ground to the east and a single-track railroad encroached close to the north and north-eastern corner. The club decided to set-up its headquarters in the 'Hyde Road Hotel' which was close-by, and important meetings were held there over the following years. The team initially changed there before and after games, a similar arrangement as was previously carried out in the 'Bulls Head Inn' at Reddish Lane.

The Hyde Road Hotel.

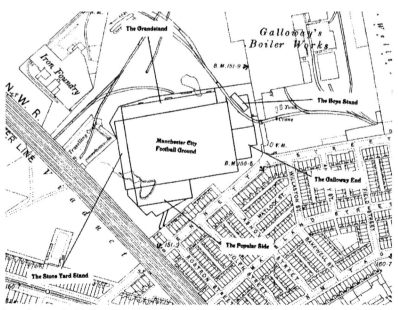

This plan of Hyde Road shows the layout of the ground following improvements in 1910. It is believed over 50,000 spectators attended here on several occasions.

Important links were made with Galloway's Works and Chester's Brewery-, who owned the Hyde Road Hotel, this enabled Ardwick AFC to make improvements to the ground. In 1888 a 1,000 capacity wooden grandstand was erected and a new entrance built on Bennett Street. This was followed in 1890 with new refreshment bars and another entrance with pathway from the side of the Hyde Road Hotel.

In 1892 Ardwick AFC were admitted to the football league as founder members of Division Two. In 1894 their demise resulted in the formation of 'Manchester City Football Club'. Further improvements continued to be made to the ground. Dressing rooms and several new turnstiles were built. Then in 1898, a syndicate was created in an attempt to buy a stand which was used for the 'Fulham Pageant'. It would cost £1,500 to transport and re-erect the stand on the site of the 1,000 capacity grandstand erected just ten years earlier. This was a far more impressive structure however, which is thought to have had a capacity of around 8,000, including 4,000 seats behind a standing paddock. The syndicate was successful and the new stand was erected in 1899. Just a year later local MP Arthur Belfour visited the ground to watch a match, he later became Prime Minister.

In 1904, FA Challenge Cup holders City spent in excess of £2,000 on improvements to Hyde Road. Stands were enlarged, access was improved and general all-round improvements raised the capacity to 40,000. These improvements turned Hyde Road into a major venue and in 1905 it hosted a cup semi-final between Newcastle United and Sheffield Wednesday.

In 1910, the three uncovered sides of the ground were roofed. The type of roofing used was multi-span, a much maligned method of cover today. The new stands were to be known as the Stone Yard Stand, capacity 2,000 seats and approximately 4,000 standing, the Popular Side, capacity approximately 17,000 standing, the Galloway End, capacity approximately

9,000 standing and incorporating a 'boys stand' in the corner behind the railway line. Hyde Road now offered cover on all sides of the ground for 35,000 spectators, with a minimum of 5,000 accommodated uncovered. This was practically unheard of at that time.

The ground had on several occasions been unable to cope with the clubs popularity. Regular disturbances and serious overcrowding had made City consider other options. Although the official record attendance at Hyde Road is 41,709, it is believed to have been surpassed on many occasions, with supporters sat on stand roofs and seen clinging to girders in an effort to see the action from above the packed crowds. The record attendance was set against Sunderland in a cup-tie in 1913. The match was eventually abandoned due to the encroachment of the crowd onto the pitch. It is thought that between 50,000 and 55,000 supporters attended Hyde Road on several occasions. The ground also witnessed two records that stand to this day. City's highest league score of 11-3 against Lincoln City on the 23rd March 1895, and Ardwick's record victory of 12-0 against Liverpool Stanley in the FA Challenge Cup 1st Qualifying Round on the 4th October 1890.

The outbreak of the First World War saw an inevitable decline in crowds as war league games and friendlies became the norm, the clubs popularity with the masses resumed in 1919 and once again City had to consider moving from the ground.

On the 27th March 1920 an historic moment in the clubs history occurred when King George V became the first reigning monarch to visit a provincial football ground. He watched as City played Liverpool and 'applauded vigorously' as City went on to win the game 2-1.

Once again the crowd at the match was recorded as being over 40,000.

Just over seven months after the Kings visit, on the evening of 6th November 1920, the Grandstand erected in 1899 was destroyed by fire.

Club records and faithful watchdog 'Nell'- an Airedale terrier, were lost in the devastation. A discarded cigarette end was later found to be the cause. The ground was quickly patched up with the help of many supporters, a new cinder banking was created and a small temporary wooden stand erected to enable the club to continue playing at Hyde Road. Official capacity was raised from 40,000 to 45,000 due to the new standing area and the absence of seats. A temporary move to Old Trafford was mooted then quickly dismissed by the clubs directors!

City wanted to move again, the board saw the fire and the impending tramway improvements which could impact on the rented ground as the perfect excuses to move and build the finest club ground in Britain, albeit away from the east of Manchester for the first time.

Football continued at Hyde Road until the end of the 1922-23 season. The final game was a practice match on the 18th August 1923, with an attendance of 10,000. The club left straight after this with the goalposts and a few turnstiles. The remaining Galloway End Stand was sold to Halifax Town for just less than £1,000 and still remains at 'The Shay'. It is now known as the 'Skircoat Stand' and is fully seated with a capacity of 2,330. All traces of the ground were gone within a decade and it was later incorporated into the bus depot, which also still stands.

As for the Hyde Road Hotel, which had a notice proudly displaying 'The Headquarters of Manchester City Football Club' for many years, the popularity of this public house diminished along with the area. It was given an unsuccessful makeover in 1983 when reopening as 'The City Gates' under landlord and former City player George Heslop. The pub eventually closed for the last time in 1988 and sadly was demolished in 2001.

A move to south Manchester beckoned for City, and a ground that was to become famous the world over lay ahead.

The Skircoat Stand, Halifax, formerly the Galloway End Stand, Hyde Road. Re-configured to form a conventional pitched roof, this structure was originally multi-spanned with a wooden roof. It was purchased from City in 1923.

Aerial photograph of the Hyde Road ground just four years after City left for Maine Road. Galloway's Works can be clearly seen along with the single-track railway and the outline of the pitch, although no stands remained.

7:   MAINE ROAD 1923-2003

It was no surprise when City announced in May 1922 that they would be leaving Hyde Road at the end of the following season. A major shock however was where they were moving to. Maine Road (Formerly 'Demesne or Dog Kennel Lane'), Moss Side, a 16.25 acre former brickwork's site purchased from the Lloyds estate for £5,500.

The newly constructed Maine Road.

Belle Vue had been the popular choice amongst supporters for the move. Several options had been proposed to the club by the Jennison family who owned the zoological gardens and its surrounding land, and City would be staying in its heartland of east Manchester. A small stadium already on the site fronting onto Hyde Road (Later to become Belle Vue Speedway and demolished in 1987), was rejected by the club because of its size limitations and the maximum lease offered by the Jennison family of just 50 years (Ardwick District- players from other local sides had joined forces with Ardwick AFC, played a charity floodlit match in aid of the Hyde Colliery disaster fund against Newton Heath here on the 26th February 1889. The attendance was 12,000 and £140 was raised for the fund).

Another site offered by the Jennison family is where the Belle Vue Greyhound Stadium was built in 1926 and still stands to this day on Kirkmanshulme Lane. Now also accommodating the Belle Vue Aces speedway team, this was Britains first greyhound stadium ever built. Once again the site did not offer enough potential and the lease was not long enough for the ambitious City directors.

Club Chairman Lawrence Furniss (Remember him at Pink Bank Lane?) instructed eminent local architect Charles Swain (Later to become a director and shareholder at the club) to design the finest club stadium in Britain on the purchased site at Maine Road. Original press reports suggested a covered grandstand with 15,000 seats and the remaining open terracing to hold 55,000. However, by the time Sir Robert McAlpine & Sons had completed the building works, the covered grandstand sat 10,000 in a single tier and the open terracing would hold 75,000. Approximate cost would be £200,000. Building took approximately sixteen months.

The new grandstand was 270ft long and 140ft wide with 54 rows of seating. It had an enormous roof with the largest span of any built at that time at a football ground. The cost of this stand alone was £120,000. Its exterior was brick with three tiled mosaics and four levels of windows to allow maximum light penetration into the clubs offices, which were housed within, and also the upper levels of the stand and stairways. Three large tunnels fronted onto the pitch, the centre one being the player's entrance. 1,700 best quality tip-up seats along with additional tip-up seating and wooden benches made up the 10,000 capacity of the stand. Inside were housed the players dressing rooms, a gymnasium, referees and linesmen rooms, various stores and heating rooms, directors rooms, the boardroom, various club offices and a reception area, kitchen, toilets and games room. Refreshment areas including bars and tea-rooms, along with toilet facilities were also accommodated within for supporter's use on matchdays.

A 1960 photograph showing the original Grandstand, Platt Lane Corner and Platt Lane Stand. The gable was originally painted with City's name.

Open terracing swept round on each side from the grandstand. The terrace was divided by a low wall and barrier approximately halfway along. In each corner were entrance/exit tunnels, which allowed supporters to enter the ground and view the pitch before deciding on their viewing point. Two tunnels were also constructed within the 'popular terrace' or supporters could if they so wished, climb the stairways at the rear of the terracing and gain access from the top, which was 106 rows high at its highest point. Total length of the terracing was equivalent to 17 miles.

The pitch was burrowed out using a steam navvy to a depth of 8ft. 3,000 tons of soil was laid on a cinder base then covered with 100-year-old fine pasture turf from Poynton.

Maine Road was officially opened on the 25th August 1923 by Lord Mayor of Manchester W. Cundiff, prior to a City match against Sheffield United. City won the 1st Division game 2-1, with the first goal being scored by City's Horace Barnes. The attendance was 58,159, a new club record. A penalty by Frank Roberts was missed during the game. The first real test of the stadiums capacity came later in that first season when on the 8th March 1924, City entertained Cardiff City in the 4th Round of the FA Cup. 76,166 people attended the match, which was a record at the time for any english match outside of London. The Empire Stadium, Wembley had opened in April 1923 to much criticism, however none of this was levelled at the new Maine Road stadium.

The 1931 Platt Lane Corner Stand after being fully seated and incorporated into the Platt Lane Stand.

The first improvements at Maine Road were carried out in 1931. The building of a covered corner stand at the Platt Lane/Grandstand end held approximately 6,800 standing and 2,000 seated spectators. This stand linked up with the Grandstand.

On the 3rd March 1934, a FA Cup 6th Round fixture against Stoke City saw the club gain unprecedented publicity. An amazing crowd of 84,569 saw City win the game 1-0. The national press were full of acclaim for the stadium, crowd and the team. Following City's victorious FA Cup campaign of 1934, the Duke of York (Future King George VI) attended the ground and watched a 1st Division match against Derby County. The attendance that day was 44,393.

Further improvements to the ground followed. A new structure known as the 'Platt Lane Stand' was erected in 1935. Five large stanchions held a roof, which linked up to the corner stand, built just 4 years earlier. The Platt Lane Stand offered covered standing accommodation until 1963 when bench seats were installed here and in the standing area in the 'Platt Lane Corner'. The new stand was opened on the 24th August 1935 and this development meant Maine Road had covered accommodation for approximately 35,000 spectators plus two large open terraced areas known as the 'Popular Side' and the 'Scoreboard End'.

During the 1940s the ground played host to Manchester United following bomb damage to Old Trafford on the 11th March 1941. United played at Maine Road until returning home in August 1949, although they did return to play three European Cup matches at the ground during season 1956-57 because they did not have floodlights erected at that time. This meant that Maine Road became the first english venue to host competitive european matches. Other clubs who have used Maine Road as a temporary home are Altrincham, Newcastle United, Northwich Victoria and Stockport County.

Floodlights were erected at Maine Road in the summer of 1953. Four pylons each 90ft high were erected and were used for the first time on the 14th October 1953 in a friendly match against Heart of Midlothian. City won 6-3 and the players wore heavy shiny shirts, which had been purchased specially so that they would stand out under the new lights. In 1957 a huge roof was constructed over the 'Popular Side', which was opposite the Grandstand. The flagpole which had flown the club flag on matchdays had to be removed from the rear of this terrace which was to be renamed the 'Kippax Stand'. This stand opened on the 4th September 1957 for a 1st Division match against Chelsea which City won 5-2. At this time City officially renamed the Grandstand the 'Main Stand'.

On the 7th May 1964 Prince Philip visited Maine Road to watch a charity match against Manchester United. Approximately 36,000 spectators attended.

The Kippax Stand and Main Stand had each been fitted with a rooftop floodlight gantry when the original four corner pylons were dismantled and sold to non-league Lockhead, of Leamington in 1964. The new 180ft pylons were installed at a cost of £36,000 and were the tallest in the football league.

In 1967 an unusual development involved the removal of the centre section of the Main Stand roof and its subsequent enlargement. The reasons for this were to install a television camera gantry and to allow the removal of two large stanchions, which held up the original roof. This development did make the stand look larger but was architecturally unimpressive. At this time the team was entering its golden age under Joe Mercer and Malcolm Allison. Fast attacking football coupled with major trophies made Maine Road the place to be unless you were supporting the opposition!

Just four years after the Main Stand roof works, the uncovered 'Scoreboard End' terrace was demolished and rebuilt as a cantilevered terrace known as the 'North Stand'. This new structure offered covered accommodation for approximately 20,000 standing spectators and incorporated refreshment bars and toilets on two levels within the stand. The original wall to the rear, constructed when the ground was built in 1923 was soonafter demolished and turnstiles were incorporated within the new North Stand. It was blue, black and grey in colour and flagpoles were erected along the front edge of the roof. To the rear a new electronic scoreboard was installed at a cost of £11,000, it was the most modern in europe and remained in use until the late 1980s when it was replaced by various new ones in the two opposite corners of the ground. The North Stand scoreboard was never removed however just covered by various painted advertisement boards. The stand had 8,120 grey tip-up seats installed in 1972, thereafter leaving the Kippax Stand as the only remaining terrace area. Capacity at this time was said to be 54,500, with Maine Road having more seating than at any other english league ground.

Aerial photograph of Maine Road showing the new North Stand and Main Stand roof extension.

The club announced a £6 million pound redevelopment plan in August 1981. New all-white 'barrel' style roofing was proposed to be erected over the Main and Kippax Stands. The North Stand would be extended around the open corner of the Kippax terrace and seated. The Platt Lane Stand would be demolished and rebuilt exactly as the North Stand opposite. The Main Stand would house a new restaurant and 36 executive boxes suspended above the touchline on a huge metal girder. These boxes would be reached via new lifts incorporated into the rear of the stand.

Phase 1 was the only part of this scheme which was ever implemented. In 1982 the Main Stand roof was removed and rebuilt at a cost of £1 million pounds but even this differed slightly from the original plans and no additional restaurant, boxes or lifts were ever constructed.

One of the three mosaics which adorned the original Grandstand at Maine Road. This was carefully removed and re-instated at the City of Manchester Stadium.

Various changes and improvements were made over the next decade as the club struggled to maintain the stadium. These included the removal of the original kippax roof floodlights and the huge 1964 floodlight pylons.

New rooftop lighting was installed to the Main and Kippax Stands. Various types of crowd control fencing was also installed then later removed.

The Main Stand façade, 1986.

In 1992, the club demolished the 1931 and 1935 Platt Lane Stands and a new structure initially named the 'Umbro Stand' after its sponsors, then renamed the 'Platt Lane Stand' was erected. It housed approximately 4,600 seats on a single tier and 48 executive boxes on two levels at the rear of the stand. A family enclosure was incorporated where the original 'Platt Lane Corner Stand' once stood. The cost of this development was said to be around £5 million pounds. It was opened on the 7th March 1993 in front of a nation-wide audience for the live televised coverage of the FA Cup Quarter-Final between City and Tottenham Hotspur. The match was marred by a pitch invasion as City lost 2-4.

A recommendation of the Taylor Report into the 1989 Hillsborough Disaster was that all top-level clubs had to have all-seater stadiums by 1994. This had encouraged City to rebuild the Platt Lane Stand earlier than would have been required and now the Kippax Stand would have to be redeveloped.

Rear view of the original Kippax Stand, 1994.

Plans for the Kippax Stand were not clear. Initially it seemed the club were to simply re-roof the stand and bolt seating onto the existing terracing. Then a two-tier stand was envisaged. Following a club take-over, new exciting plans for the complete demolition of the kippax and erection of a three-tier 11,000 capacity stand incorporating 32 executive boxes, refreshment bars and glass fronted restaurants overlooking the pitch on the upper-tier were announced. This new Kippax Stand would cost £10 million pounds and at 100ft high would tower over the other three sides of the ground.

The original and much loved 1957 Kippax Stand, which was home to the clubs most fervent and vocal supporters, was demolished following City's 2-2 draw with Chelsea on the 30th April 1994. It was the largest terraced stand still open at any english league ground at this time. The attendance at this 1st Division match was 33,594.

The 1957 Kippax Stand on its last day with rooftop floodlighting.

The new stand was completed in phases and officially opened by former City favourite Bert Trautmann during 1995.

Aerial view of Maine Road, 1997.

This stand became the last significant development at Maine Road, although temporary seating was installed in both the open corners of the Kippax Stand and available areas in the Platt Lane and Main Stand. This enabled the ground to have a final all-seated capacity of 35,150.

The development of Maine Road was done on a piece-meal basis; although the 1995 completed Kippax Stand did have a feasible development plan to extend around the other three sides of the ground. The earlier 1981 plan could also have worked successfully.

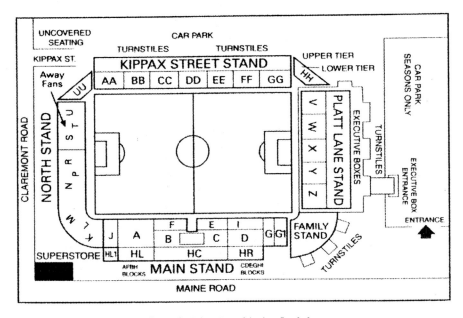

Plan of Maine Road in its final days.

When the club played its last match at the ground on the 11th May 2003, an emotional 0-1 Premier League defeat against Southampton in front of 34,957 supporters, approximately a dozen of the turnstiles taken from Hyde Road were still in operation.

The 'barrel' style all-white 1982 Main Stand roof and North Stand.

Originally the Umbro Stand, later the Platt Lane Stand after its predecessor.

The Main Stand façade, 2003.

Rear view of the Kippax Stand 2003, also shows temporary uncovered corner seating.

It had been envisaged that Sale Sharks Rugby Union Club would become tenants following City's departure but the size of the ground in comparison to the 'Sharks' small attendance's did not make this viable. Stockport County Football Club also declared an interest in moving into the ground but Manchester City Council refused them permission to do so.

An auction was held to sell off various items from the ground, raising approximately £100,000. By spring 2004 Maine Road was completely demolished and cleared, with various plans already being discussed to redevelop the site for housing.

The last City player to score at Maine Road was Marc-Vivien Foe who tragically died before the club kicked a ball at its new home. The ground played host to seventeen FA Cup Semi-Finals, five of them replays, five League Cup Semi-Finals, two European Cup Winners Cup Semi-Finals and a Football League Cup Final Replay in 1984. It hosted four England Internationals including an 8-0 victory against Scotland in 1943, and a 9-2 victory against Ireland in 1949 (This was the first World Cup qualifier to be held at an english venue and doubled as a home international). Various league representative matches, England B, Under 23, Under 21 and amateur matches were also held there. Other events include numerous pop concerts, eleven rugby league championship play-off finals, rugby league matches and a dual code rugby challenge match. Professional tennis, Jehovah's Witnesses meetings, evangelical meetings and even the world's largest carol concert was held at Maine Road in 2002.

As for City, just like 1923 they were again moving into the finest club stadium in Britain.

In 1985 the 'Manchester Olympic Bid Committee' was formed and two bids were made to host the Olympic Games. The first bid was based around a plan to redevelop a site to the west of the city in the Eccles area, and proposed the building of an 80,000 all-seater, multi-purpose athletics stadium. When Atlanta, USA was successful with the 1996 games bid, the plan was immediately scrapped.

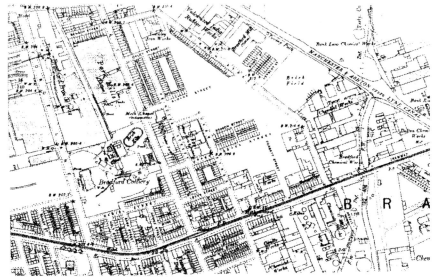

Map of the City of Manchester Stadium site. Heavily industrialised and remaining so for the next 100 years.

The second bid was for the 2000 Olympic Games, and focus switched to the Bradford area of east Manchester, which was once heavily industrialised but suffered serious economic decline in the 1970s and 1980s. The city council was granted £70 million pounds from central government to compulsory purchase land and clear the site where a stadium was to be built. New facilities were constructed such as an indoor arena and concert hall in Manchester city centre, and a cycling velodrome close to the proposed stadium site at the renamed 'Eastlands' area.

Manchester lost again however, this time to Sydney, Australia. In reality it was no contest, but the redevelopment of Eastlands was underway and when the city council scaled down its ambitions and successfully bid for the 2002 Commonwealth Games, the excitement in Manchester was at a height.

Manchester United FC said that they had spent too much on the redevelopment of its Old Trafford ground to ever move away, but City had always said it was prepared to negotiate with the council on the building of a new stadium. Despite heavy recent spending on its Maine Road ground, the club knew that if a permanent stadium was to be built for the games then they were the only ones who could fill it to its capacity on a regular basis.

The original plan for the Commonwealth Games stadium was for a multi-purpose 60,000 seat stadium with a running track. The council were desperate not to build a temporary structure but wanted a permanent legacy for the city following the games, therefore a tenant was required to give the stadium a sustainable future.

Following lengthy negotiations City, led by Chairman David Bernstein, agreed to move into the new stadium after the commonwealth games ended if certain conditions were met. These included that the stadium would have no running track but seating to pitch level and the club given sole rights as tenants to the stadium, therefore a new home in every sense of the word. This would mean a revised plan being conceived where the stadium would be partially built to a capacity of 38,000 for the games, including one open temporary stand at the north end of the stadium. It would then be converted into a football stadium with a capacity of 48,000 for Manchester City to play in from season 2003-04. This would mean the running track being removed and its base dug out to provide an extra tier of seating to pitch level and a new north stand being built to complete the stadium.

Aerial photograph of the City of Manchester Stadium site, 1928.

Surprisingly the city council agreed to the plan, and much criticism followed from the athletics community and city financiers who could not believe what was happening, basically that the football club were having a new state-of-the-art stadium built for them at no charge by the government and city council. The athletics community felt that a top class arena was required in Britain for track and field events and saw the stadium being given away to a football club with its own ground already well established.

Nevertheless, with £77 million pounds being committed by Sport England and the city council providing the remainder, the £110 million pound stadium was destined to be built. 'Ove Arup' were charged with the stadium whilst 'Laing' did the actual work. Laing actually constructed the 'barrel' style roof on City's Main Stand back in 1982.

The bowl shaped design of the stadium was breathtaking and featured twelve distinctive 60m high masts and a suspended rim cable-stayed roof. The shape of the roof was chosen to guarantee an excellent view for each spectator, provide maximum shelter from Manchester's inclement

45

weather and amplify the noise of the crowd. The track would be laid with concrete terracing underneath ready to be converted to a seated tier following the games.

City of Manchester Stadium under construction, October 2000.

Temporary North Stand under construction, February 2002.

The construction work began and Prime Minister Tony Blair laid the foundation stone in December 1999. It took the 3,000 strong workforce 27 months to complete and the stadium was handed over to delighted games organisers on the 21st March 2002. It soon hosted its first competitive event just two months later- the North of England Junior Championships.

XVII Commonwealth Games Opening Ceremony, 25th July 2002.

The stadium was officially opened by Queen Elizabeth II on the 25th July 2002, at the opening ceremony of the XVII Commonwealth Games. Her Majesty also attended the closing ceremony on the 4th August 2002, accompanied on both occasions by Prince Philip. The games were an outstanding success, which gained world-wide acclaim, with many people who doubted whether Manchester would be capable of hosting such an event left open-mouthed. Immediately following the games work began on transforming the stadium into a new home for the football club. The running track was removed and re-laid in Birmingham. The temporary North Stand was dismantled and a permanent stand was built to complete the original plan of the stadium. Work was again completed on time and

City invested several million pounds on upgrading the stadium facilities for its supporters. City negotiated a one hundred years lease on the stadium and Maine Road went into city council ownership as soon as the club moved into its new home.

The club's opening fixture was a friendly against Barcelona on the 10th August 2003. City won 2-1 with Nicolas Anelka scoring the first goal. Attendance was a permitted maximum of 36,518. The clubs highest attendance to date at the City of Manchester Stadium is 47,304 against Chelsea on the 28th February 2004, in the Premier League.

View from the North Stand prior to City's opening fixture at the City of Manchester Stadium.

Aerial view of the City of Manchester Stadium.

The capacity of the City of Manchester Stadium is 47,540, broken down as follows:

Colin Bell Stand (West)	Level 3	5,275
	Level 2	4,381
	Level 1	5,663
East Stand	Level 3	5,331
	Level 2	4,356
	Level 1	6,481
Family Stand (North)	Level 2	3,586
North Stand	Level 1	4,427
Key 103 Stand (South)	Level 2	3,600
	Level 1	4,440
Level 3 Capacity		10,606
Level 2 Capacity		15,923
Level 1 Capacity		21,011

The stadium incorporates approximately 300 seats for disabled spectators at various levels including match commentary via headsets for blind persons.

The concourses provide seating and standing areas with hot food, beverage, sweets, merchandising, vending and betting facilities. Match action from previous and current games is relayed to flat widescreen TVs throughout the concourse areas before, during and after the match.

Sixty-nine hospitality boxes seat between 8 and 22 guests. There are seven function suites: The Boardroom Suite, The Mancunian, Legends Lounge, Citizens Suite, 1894 Suite and The Commonwealth Suite have capacities of between 120 to 420 guests. At the north end of the stadium is the clubs superstore, museum and another suite named the City Social Café.

Stadium capacity could be expanded to approximately 56,000 seated spectators by extending the upper tier (level 3) around both ends of the stadium and raising the roof. Although initial costs would be high it was built with this possible development incorporated into its design and structure. Manchester City FC would have to meet the full cost of any future expansion.

Supporters access to the stadium is via 86 electronically activated swipecard gates. Access to the stadium for visiting teams and emergency vehicles is via an underground tunnel at the north-western corner of the stadium, near to the Regional Athletics Arena where City's reserve team now plays its fixtures. This arena, complete with a running track has covered accommodation for 6,000 seated spectators.

Various sculptures and monuments adorn the surroundings of the stadium, most notably the largest sculpture in Britain known as the 'B of the Bang' at the south-eastern corner. In the clubs memorial garden near to the Colin Bell Stand main entrance, a tiled mosaic which was originally on the Grandstand façade at Maine Road has been lovingly re-instated and some ornate brickwork from the Hyde Road Hotel is also on display.

Tiled mosaic paying homage to Joe Mercer OBE, on display at the north end of the City of Manchester Stadium.

The stadium has already played host to pop concerts, an international football tournament with England, Iceland and Japan taking part, a Great Britain v Australia Rugby League Tri-Nations Tournament match and a UEFA European Women's Championship football match.

The journey from Clowes Street has been a long and interesting one for Manchester City.

ATTENDANCE RECORDS

Highest attendance:

84,569 v Stoke City, FA Cup 6th Round, 3rd March 1934 (Maine Road).

A record for any provincial game in Britain.

Highest league attendance:

83,260 Manchester United v Arsenal, Division 1, 17th January 1948 (Maine Road).

A record for any English league match and Manchester Uniteds highest in any home match.

Highest aggregate league attendance:

In 1947-48 season 2,049,915 spectators attended City and United home league matches at Maine Road. A record for any British ground.

Highest midweek FA Cup attendance (Other than a final):

80,407 Birmingham City v Derby County, FA Cup Semi-Final Replay, 28th March 1946
(Maine Road).

Highest league attendance for a City home match:

79,491 v Arsenal, Division 1, 23rd February 1935 (Maine Road).

Highest attendance for a match involving a non-league team:

81,565 Manchester United v Yeovil, FA Cup 5th Round, 12th February 1949 (Maine Road).

A record for any English provincial match involving a non-league team.

Highest post-war attendance for a Women's match in Europe:

29,092 England v Finland, UEFA European Women's Championship Group A, 5th June 2005 (City of Manchester Stadium).

A record attendance for any UEFA European Women's Championship match.

AVERAGE HOME LEAGUE ATTENDANCES

1880-91 .... No detailed records available
1891-92 6,800
1892-93 3,000
1893-94 4,000
1894-95 6,000
1895-96 10,000
1896-97 8,000
1897-98 8,000
1898-99 10,000
1899-1900 16,000
1900-01 18,300
1901-02 17,000
1902-03 16,000
1903-04 20,000
1904-05 20,000
1905-06 18,000
1906-07 22,150
1907-08 23,000
1908-09 20,000
1909-10 18,275
1910-11 26,000
1911-12 24,625
1912-13 24,000
1913-14 27,000
1914-15 21,000
1915-16 10,600
1916-17 10,000
1917-18 12,200
1918-19 15,700
1919-20 25,240

1920-21	31,020
1921-22	25,000
1922-23	24,000
1923-24	27,400
1924-25	29,000
1925-26	32,000
1926-27	30,848
1927-28	37,468
1928-29	31,715
1929-30	33,339
1930-31	26,849
1931-32	24,173
1932-33	24,254
1933-34	30,058
1934-35	34,824
1935-36	33,577
1936-37	35,872
1937-38	32,670
1938-39	31,291
1939-40	4,100
1940-41	4,000
1941-42	4,900
1942-43	10,900
1943-44	14,200
1944-45	15,400
1945-46	24,000
1946-47	39,283
1947-48	42,725
1948-49	38,699
1949-50	39,381
1950-51	35,016
1951-52	38,302
1952-53	34,663

1953-54.. 30,155

1954-55.. 35,217

1955-56.. 32,198

1956-57.. 30,005

1957-58.. 32,765

1958-59.. 32,568

1959-60.. 35,637

1960-61.. 29,409

1961-62.. 25,626

1962-63.. 24,683

1963-64.. 18,201

1964-65.. 14,753

1965-66.. 27,739

1966-67.. 31,209

1967-68.. 37,223

1968-69.. 33,750

1969-70.. 33,930

1970-71.. 31,041

1971-72.. 38,573

1972-73.. 32,351

1973-74.. 30,756

1974-75.. 32,898

1975-76.. 34,281

1976-77.. 40,058

1977-78.. 41,687

1978-79.. 36,203

1979-80.. 35,272

1980-81.. 33,587

1981-82.. 34,063

1982-83.. 26,789

1983-84.. 25,604

1984-85.. 24,220

1985-86.. 24,229

1986-87	21,922
1987-88	19,471
1988-89	23,500
1989-90	27,975
1990-91	27,874
1991-92	27,691
1992-93	24,698
1993-94	26,709
1994-95	22,725
1995-96	27,829
1996-97	26,753
1997-98	28,196
1998-99	28,261
1999-2000	32,088
2000-01	34,058
2001-02	33,059
2002-03	34,564
2003-04	46,834
2004-05	45,192

Please note:

Prior to season 1892-93 the club was not in the football league.

Seasons 1915-16 to 1918-19 and 1939-40 to 1945-46 inclusive, the club was playing war league matches.

LIST OF MAPS & ILLUSTRATIONS

Maps

1   St Marks Church and Clowes Street, West Gorton, 1893.
     The site of the pitch was adjacent to the Union Iron Works.

2   The locations of three grounds are visible on this map of the Belle
     Vue area of Gorton, 1893. The Kirkmanshulme Cricket Club (1),
     Queens Road (2) and Pink Bank Lane (3) grounds. Note also the
     running track, which became the speedway stadium.

3   Reddish Lane showing the location of the Bulls Head Inn, 1893.
     The football ground is believed to have been beside this public
     house.

4   This plan of Hyde Road shows the layout of the ground following
     improvements in 1910. It is believed over 50,000 spectators
     attended here on several occasions.

5   Plan of Maine Road in its final days.

6   Map of the City of Manchester Stadium site. Heavily industrialised
     and remaining so for the next 100 years.

Illustrations

1   St Marks Church, Clowes Street, West Gorton

2   Aerial photograph dated 1937 showing the site of Kirkmanshulme Cricket Club, Queens Road ground, Greenwood House flats on Pink Bank Lane, Belle Vue Speedway stadium and Belle Vue Greyhound stadium.

3   Gorton Park, formerly Clemington Park or Donkey Common. This was the Queens Road ground.

4   Aerial photograph taken in 1926. Pink Bank Lane ground is at the bottom right.
Note the Speedway Stadium compared to the 1937 photograph.

5   City 2 Middlesbrough 1, at Hyde Road, 14th April 1911. Note the multi-spanned roof.

6   The Hyde Road Hotel.

7   The Skircoat Stand, Halifax, formerly the Galloway End Stand, Hyde Road.
Re-configured to form a conventional pitched roof, this structure was originally multi-spanned with a wooden roof. It was purchased from City in 1923.

8   Aerial photograph of the Hyde Road ground just four years after City left for Maine Road. Galloway's Works can be clearly seen along with the single-track railway and the outline of the pitch, although no stands remained.

9   The newly constructed Maine Road.

10   A 1960 photograph showing the original Grandstand, Platt Lane Corner and Platt Lane Stand. The gable was originally painted with City's name.

11   The 1931 Platt Lane Corner Stand after being fully seated and incorporated into the Platt Lane Stand.

12   Aerial photograph of Maine Road showing the new North Stand and Main Stand roof extension.

13   One of the three mosaics which adorned the original Grandstand at Maine Road. This was carefully removed and re-instated at the City of Manchester Stadium.

14   The Main Stand façade, 1986.

15   Rear view of the original Kippax Stand, 1994.

16   The 1957 Kippax Stand on its last day with rooftop floodlighting.

17   Aerial view of Maine Road, 1997.

18   The 'barrel' style all-white 1982 Main Stand roof and North Stand.

19   Originally the Umbro Stand, later the Platt Lane Stand after its predecessor.

20   The Main Stand façade, 2003.

21   Rear view of the Kippax Stand 2003, also shows temporary uncovered corner seating.

ACKNOWLEDGEMENTS

My thanks to the following sources for photographs, maps, information
and inspiration:

Manchester Archives and Local Studies
Simmons Aerofilms
MCFC Souvenir History~ Fred Johnson
The Football Grounds of Great Britain~ Simon Inglis
MCFC Football Book No 1~ Peter Gardner
The Manchester City Story~ Andrew Ward
Manchester City- A Complete Record 1887-1987~ Ray Goble
Manchester The Greatest City~ Gary James
Farewell to Maine Road~ Gary James
MCFC Official Record Handbook~ Bill Miles
A-Z of Manchester Football~ Derek Brandon
Manchester City Centenary Brochure~ MCFC
Manchester City FC Match Magazines~ MCFC

David Burton   (July 2005)

Printed in the United Kingdom
by Lightning Source UK Ltd.
107525UKS00002BA/1-4